MznLnx

Missing Links Exam Preps

Exam Prep for

Professional Selling: A Trust-Based Approach

Ingram et al..., 3rd Edition

The MznLnx Exam Prep is your link from the texbook and lecture to your exams.
The MznLnx Exam Preps are unauthorized and comprehensive reviews of your textbooks.

MznLnx

Rico
Publications

Exam Prep for Professional Selling: A Trust-Based Approach
3rd Edition
Ingram et al...

Publisher: Raymond Houge
Assistant Editor: Michael Rouger
Text and Cover Designer: Lisa Buckner
Marketing Manager: Sara Swagger
Project Manager, Editorial Production: Jerry Emerson
Art Director: Vernon Lowerui

Product Manager: Dave Mason
Editorial Assitant: Rachel Guzmanji
Pedagogy: Debra Long
Cover Image: Jim Reed/Getty Images
Text and Cover Printer: City Printing, Inc.
Compositor: Media Mix, Inc.

For more information about our products, contact us at:
Dave.Mason@RicoPublications.com

For permission to use material from this text or product, submit a request online to:
Dave.Mason@RicoPublications.com

Printed in the United States
ISBN:

Contents

TO THE STUDENT

COMPREHENSIVE

The *MznLnx* Exam Prep series is designed to help you pass your exams. Editors at MznLnx review your textbooks and then prepare these practice exams to help you master the textbook material. Unlike study guides, workbooks, and practice tests provided by the texbook publisher and textbook authors, *MznLnx* gives you ***all*** of the material in each chapter in exam form, not just samples, so you can be sure to nail your exam.

MECHANICAL

The MznLnx Exam Prep series creates exams that will help you learn the subject matter as well as test you on your understanding. Each question is designed to help you master the concept. Just working through the exams, you gain an understanding of the subject--its a simple mechanical process that produces success.

INTEGRATED STUDY GUIDE AND REVIEW

MznLnx is not just a set of exams designed to test you, its also a comprehensive review of the subject content. Each exam question is also a review of the concept, making sure that you will get the answer correct without having to go to other sources of material. You learn as you go! Its the easiest way to pass an exam.

HUMOR

Studying can be tedious and dry. MznLnx's instructional design includes moderate humor within the exam questions on occassion, to break the tedium and revitalize the brain

1. _________ is an advertisement in which a particular product specifically mentions a competitor by name for the express purpose of showing why the competitor is inferior to the product naming it.

This should not be confused with parody advertisements, where a fictional product is being advertised for the purpose of poking fun at the particular advertisement, nor should it be confused with the use of a coined brand name for the purpose of comparing the product without actually naming an actual competitor. ('Wikipedia tastes better and is less filling than the Encyclopedia Galactica.')

In the 1980s, during what has been referred to as the cola wars, soft-drink manufacturer Pepsi ran a series of advertisements where people, caught on hidden camera, in a blind taste test, chose Pepsi over rival Coca-Cola.

a. Cost per conversion
b. Comparative advertising
c. Heavy-up
d. GL-70

2. The _________ was a worldwide economic downturn starting in most places in 1929 and ending at different times in the 1930s or early 1940s for different countries. It was the largest and most important economic depression in the 20th century, and is used in the 21st century as an example of how far the world's economy can fall. The _________ originated in the United States; historians most often use as a starting date the stock market crash on October 29, 1929, known as Black Tuesday.

a. 6-3-5 Brainwriting
b. 180SearchAssistant
c. Power III
d. Great Depression

3. The _________ is a professional association for marketers. As of 2008 it had approximately 40,000 members. There are collegiate chapters on 250 campuses.

a. ACNielsen
b. AMAX
c. ADTECH
d. American Marketing Association

4. _________ is a branch of philosophy which seeks to address questions about morality, such as how a moral outcome can be achieved in a specific situation (applied _________), how moral values should be determined (normative _________), what moral values people actually abide by (descriptive _________), what the fundamental semantic, ontological, and epistemic nature of _________ or morality is (meta-_________), and how moral capacity or moral agency develops and what its nature is (moral psychology.)

Socrates was one of the first Greek philosophers to encourage both scholars and the common citizen to turn their attention from the outside world to the condition of man. In this view, Knowledge having a bearing on human life was placed highest, all other knowledge being secondary.

a. AMAX
b. ADTECH
c. Ethics
d. ACNielsen

5. _________ is defined by the American _________ Association as the activity, set of institutions, and processes for creating, communicating, delivering, and exchanging offerings that have value for customers, clients, partners, and society at large. The term developed from the original meaning which referred literally to going to market, as in shopping, or going to a market to sell goods or services.

_________ practice tends to be seen as a creative industry, which includes advertising, distribution and selling.

a. Customer acquisition management
b. Marketing
c. Product naming
d. Marketing myopia

6. _________ is the process by which a new idea or new product is accepted by the market. The rate of _________ is the speed that the new idea spreads from one consumer to the next. Adoption is similar to _________ except that it deals with the psychological processes an individual goes through, rather than an aggregate market process.
a. Kano model
b. Perceptual maps
c. Diffusion
d. Market development

7. _________ is a theory of how, why, and at what rate new ideas and technology spread through cultures. Everett Rogers introduced it in his 1962 book, _________s, writing that 'Diffusion is the process by which an innovation is communicated through certain channels over time among the members of a social system.' The adoption curve becomes an s-curve when cumulative adoption is used.

Rogers theorized that innovations would spread through a community in an S curve, as the early adopters select the innovation (which may be a technology) first, followed by the majority, until a technology or innovation has reached its saturation point in a community.

According to Rogers, diffusion research centers on the conditions which increase or decrease the likelihood that a new idea, product, or practice will be adopted by members of a given culture.

a. Diffusion of innovation
b. 180SearchAssistant
c. Power III
d. 6-3-5 Brainwriting

8. _________s is the social science that studies the production, distribution, and consumption of goods and services. The term _________s comes from the Ancient Greek oá¼°κονομÎ¯α from oá¼¶κος (oikos, 'house') + vÏŒμος (nomos, 'custom' or 'law'), hence 'rules of the house(hold)'. Current _________ models developed out of the broader field of political economy in the late 19th century, owing to a desire to use an empirical approach more akin to the physical sciences.

a. ACNielsen
b. Industrial organization
c. ADTECH
d. Economic

9. _________ describes the situation when output from (or information about the result of) an event or phenomenon in the past will influence the same event/phenomenon in the present or future. When an event is part of a chain of cause-and-effect that forms a circuit or loop, then the event is said to 'feed back' into itself.

_________ is also a synonym for:

- _________ Signal; the information about the initial event that is the basis for subsequent modification of the event.
- _________ Loop; the causal path that leads from the initial generation of the _________ signal to the subsequent modification of the event.

_________ is a mechanism, process or signal that is looped back to control a system within itself. Such a loop is called a _________ loop.

a. Feedback
b. 6-3-5 Brainwriting
c. Power III
d. 180SearchAssistant

10. _________ often refers to either primary or secondary research. Secondary research involves a company using information compiled from various sources, which is about a new or existing product. The advantages of secondary research are that it is relatively cheap and easily accessible.

a. Market research
b. Mystery shoppers
c. Questionnaire
d. Mystery shopping

11. _________ is the provision of service to customers before, during and after a purchase.

According to Turban et al., '_________ is a series of activities designed to enhance the level of customer satisfaction - that is, the feeling that a product or service has met the customer expectation.'

Its importance varies by product, industry and customer.

a. Customer experience
b. COPC Inc.
c. Facing
d. Customer service

12. _________ is a measure of the strength of a brand, product, service relative to competitive offerings. There is often a geographic element to the competitive landscape. In defining _________, you must see to what extent a product, brand, or firm controls a product category in a given geographic area.

a. Market system
b. Discretionary spending
c. Productivity
d. Market dominance

13. The term _________ was first coined by New York Times best selling author, Linda Richardson. _________ emphasizes customer needs and meeting those needs with solutions combining products and/or services. A consultative salesperson typically provides detailed instruction or advice on which solution best meets these needs.

a. Request for proposal
b. Lead generation
c. Sales management
d. Consultative selling

14. In economic models, the _________ time frame assumes no fixed factors of production. Firms can enter or leave the marketplace, and the cost (and availability) of land, labor, raw materials, and capital goods can be assumed to vary. In contrast, in the short-run time frame, certain factors are assumed to be fixed, because there is not sufficient time for them to change.

a. 180SearchAssistant
b. 6-3-5 Brainwriting
c. Power III
d. Long-run

15. A _________ is a systematic approach to selling a product or service. A growing body of published literature approaches the _________ from the point of view of an engineering discipline

Reasons for having a well thought-out _________ include seller and buyer risk management, standardized customer interaction in sales, and scalable revenue generation.

a. Sales management
b. Request for proposal
c. Lead generation
d. Sales process

16. A personal and cultural _________ is a relative ethic _________, an assumption upon which implementation can be extrapolated. A _________ system is a set of consistent _________s and measures that is soo not true. A principle _________ is a foundation upon which other _________s and measures of integrity are based.

a. Package-on-Package
b. Perceptual maps
c. Supreme Court of the United States
d. Value

17. The _________ is a very large set of interlinked hypertext documents accessed via the Internet. With a Web browser, one can view Web pages that may contain text, images, videos, and other multimedia and navigate between them using hyperlinks. Using concepts from earlier hypertext systems, the _________ was begun in 1992 by the English physicist Sir Tim Berners-Lee, now the Director of the _________ Consortium, and Robert Cailliau, a Belgian computer scientist, while both were working at CERN in Geneva, Switzerland.

a. Power III
b. 6-3-5 Brainwriting
c. 180SearchAssistant
d. World Wide Web

18. _________ is a range of services providing assistance with technology products such as mobile phones, televisions, computers, or other electronic or mechanical goods. In general, _________ services attempt to help the user solve specific problems with a product--rather than providing training, customization, or other support services.

Most companies offer _________ for the products they sell, either freely available or for a fee.

a. 6-3-5 Brainwriting
b. 180SearchAssistant
c. Technical support
d. Power III

19. _________ is defined by communication scholars in numerous ways, usually describing participants who are dependent upon one another and have a shared history. Communication channels, the conceptualization of mediums that carry messages from sender to receiver, take two distinct forms: direct and indirect.

Direct channels are obvious and easily recognized by the receiver.

a. ACNielsen
b. AMAX
c. ADTECH
d. Interpersonal communication

20. _________ is a business discipline which is focused on the practical application of marketing techniques and the management of a firm's marketing resources and activities. Marketing managers are often responsible for influencing the level, timing, and composition of customer demand accepted definition of the term. In part, this is because the role of a marketing manager can vary significantly based on a business' size, corporate culture, and industry context.
a. Marketing Management
b. Business structure
c. Performance-based advertising
d. Door-to-door

21. _________ is the set of reasons that determines one to engage in a particular behavior. The term is generally used for human _________ but, theoretically, it can be used to describe the causes for animal behavior as well
a. 180SearchAssistant
b. Role playing
c. Power III
d. Motivation

1. The _________ is a professional association for marketers. As of 2008 it had approximately 40,000 members. There are collegiate chapters on 250 campuses.

a. ADTECH
b. American Marketing Association
c. ACNielsen
d. AMAX

2. _________ is defined by the American _________ Association as the activity, set of institutions, and processes for creating, communicating, delivering, and exchanging offerings that have value for customers, clients, partners, and society at large. The term developed from the original meaning which referred literally to going to market, as in shopping, or going to a market to sell goods or services.

_________ practice tends to be seen as a creative industry, which includes advertising, distribution and selling.

a. Marketing myopia
b. Product naming
c. Marketing
d. Customer acquisition management

3. _________ is a branch of philosophy which seeks to address questions about morality, such as how a moral outcome can be achieved in a specific situation (applied _________), how moral values should be determined (normative _________), what moral values people actually abide by (descriptive _________), what the fundamental semantic, ontological, and epistemic nature of _________ or morality is (meta-_________), and how moral capacity or moral agency develops and what its nature is (moral psychology.)

Socrates was one of the first Greek philosophers to encourage both scholars and the common citizen to turn their attention from the outside world to the condition of man. In this view, Knowledge having a bearing on human life was placed highest, all other knowledge being secondary.

a. ADTECH
b. AMAX
c. ACNielsen
d. Ethics

4. _________ has been defined by the International Organization for Standardization (ISO) as 'ensuring that information is accessible only to those authorized to have access' and is one of the cornerstones of information security. _________ is one of the design goals for many cryptosystems, made possible in practice by the techniques of modern cryptography.

_________ also refers to an ethical principle associated with several professions (e.g., medicine, law, religion, professional psychology, and journalism.)

a. 180SearchAssistant
b. Confidentiality
c. 6-3-5 Brainwriting
d. Power III

5. _________ is a value showing the reliability of a person to others because of his/her integrity, truthfulness, and trustfulness, traits that can encourage someone to depend on him/her.

The wider use of this noun is in Systems engineering.

_________ as applied to a computer system is defined by the IFIP 10.4 Working Group on Dependable Computing and Fault Tolerance as:

> '[..] the trustworthiness of a computing system which allows reliance to be justifiably placed on the service it delivers [..]'

an alternative and broader definition is provided by IEC IEV 191-02-03:

> '_________ the collective term used to describe the availability performance and its influencing factors : reliability performance, maintainability performance and maintenance support performance'

This concept can be further extended to encompass mechanisms to increase and maintain the _________ of a system .

a. 6-3-5 Brainwriting
b. 180SearchAssistant
c. Dependability
d. Power III

6. _________ is the degree to which a correct prediction or forecast of a system's state can be made either qualitatively or quantitatively. Although the second law of thermodynamics can tell us about the equilibrium state that a system will evolve to, and steady states in dissipative systems can sometimes be predicted, there exists no general rule to predict the time evolution of systems far from equilibrium, e.g. chaotic systems, if they do not approach some kind of equilibrium. Their _________ usually deteriorates with time.

a. 6-3-5 Brainwriting
b. Power III
c. 180SearchAssistant
d. Predictability

7. An _________ is the manufacturing of a good or service within a category. Although _________ is a broad term for any kind of economic production, in economics and urban planning _________ is a synonym for the secondary sector, which is a type of economic activity involved in the manufacturing of raw materials into goods and products.

There are four key industrial economic sectors: the primary sector, largely raw material extraction industries such as mining and farming; the secondary sector, involving refining, construction, and manufacturing; the tertiary sector, which deals with services (such as law and medicine) and distribution of manufactured goods; and the quaternary sector, a relatively new type of knowledge _________ focusing on technological research, design and development such as computer programming, and biochemistry.

a. ACNielsen
b. Industry
c. ADTECH
d. AMAX

8. _________ in economics and business is the result of an exchange and from that trade we assign a numerical monetary value to a good, service or asset. If I trade 4 apples for an orange, the _________ of an orange is 4 - apples. Inversely, the _________ of an apple is 1/4 oranges.

a. Price
b. Contribution margin-based pricing
c. Discounts and allowances
d. Pricing

9. _________ involves disseminating information about a product, product line, brand, or company. It is one of the four key aspects of the marketing mix. (The other three elements are product marketing, pricing, and distribution). P>_________ is generally sub-divided into two parts.

- Above the line _________: Promotion in the media (e.g. TV, radio, newspapers, Internet and Mobile Phones) in which the advertiser pays an advertising agency to place the ad
- Below the line _________: All other _________. Much of this is intended to be subtle enough for the consumer to be unaware that _________ is taking place. E.g. sponsorship, product placement, endorsements, sales _________, merchandising, direct mail, personal selling, public relations, trade shows

a. Cashmere Agency
b. Promotion
c. Davie Brown Index
d. Bottling lines

10. _________ is an advertisement in which a particular product specifically mentions a competitor by name for the express purpose of showing why the competitor is inferior to the product naming it.

This should not be confused with parody advertisements, where a fictional product is being advertised for the purpose of poking fun at the particular advertisement, nor should it be confused with the use of a coined brand name for the purpose of comparing the product without actually naming an actual competitor. ('Wikipedia tastes better and is less filling than the Encyclopedia Galactica.')

In the 1980s, during what has been referred to as the cola wars, soft-drink manufacturer Pepsi ran a series of advertisements where people, caught on hidden camera, in a blind taste test, chose Pepsi over rival Coca-Cola.

a. Comparative advertising
b. GL-70
c. Heavy-up
d. Cost per conversion

11. _________ is the provision of service to customers before, during and after a purchase.

According to Turban et al., '_________ is a series of activities designed to enhance the level of customer satisfaction - that is, the feeling that a product or service has met the customer expectation.'

Its importance varies by product, industry and customer.

a. Customer experience
b. Facing
c. Customer service
d. COPC Inc.

12. _________ is the practice of individuals including commercial businesses, governments and institutions, facilitating the sale of their products or services to other companies or organizations that in turn resell them, use them as components in products or services they offer _________ is also called business-to-_________ for short. (Note that while marketing to government entities shares some of the same dynamics of organizational marketing, B2G Marketing is meaningfully different.)

a. Business marketing
b. Law of disruption
c. Disruptive technology
d. Mass marketing

13. In accounting, _________ has a very specific meaning. It is an outflow of cash or other valuable assets from a person or company to another person or company. This outflow of cash is generally one side of a trade for products or services that have equal or better current or future value to the buyer than to the seller.

a. AMAX
b. ADTECH
c. ACNielsen
d. Expense

14. An _________ is quite usually a standard guarantee from the seller of a product that specifies the extent to which the quality or performance of the product is assured and states the conditions under which the product can be returned, replaced, or repaired. It is often given in the form of a specific, written 'Warranty' document. However, a warranty may also arise by operation of law based upon the seller's description of the goods, and perhaps their source and quality, and any material deviation from that specification would violate the guarantee.
a. Office for Harmonization in the Internal Market
b. Imperial Group v. Philip Morris
c. Energy Star
d. Express warranty

15. In the social sciences, a _________ is a society where valuable goods and services are regularly given without any explicit agreement for immediate or future rewards (i.e. there is no visible quid pro quo). Ideally, simultaneous or recurring giving serves to circulate and redistribute valuables within the community. The organization of a _________ stands in contrast to a barter economy or a market economy.
a. Protectionism
b. Mixed economy
c. Black market
d. Gift economy

16. _________ is the area of law in which manufacturers, distributors, suppliers, retailers, and others who make products available to the public are held responsible for the injuries those products cause.

In the United States, the claims most commonly associated with _________ are negligence, strict liability, breach of warranty, and various consumer protection claims. The majority of _________ laws are determined at the state level and vary widely from state to state.

a. Registered trademark symbol
b. Trespass to land
c. Mediation
d. Product liability

17. In economics, _________ is the desire to own something and the ability to pay for it. The term _________ signifies the ability or the willingness to buy a particular commodity at a given point of time .

.

a. Discretionary spending
b. Market dominance
c. Market system
d. Demand

1. _________ is a broad label that refers to any individuals or households that use goods and services generated within the economy. The concept of a _________ is used in different contexts, so that the usage and significance of the term may vary.

A _________ is a person who uses any product or service.

a. Power III
b. 180SearchAssistant
c. 6-3-5 Brainwriting
d. Consumer

2. _________ is a term in economics, where demand for one good or service occurs as a result of demand for another. This may occur as the former is a part of production of the second. For example, demand for coal leads to _________ for mining, as coal must be mined for coal to be consumed.

a. 6-3-5 Brainwriting
b. 180SearchAssistant
c. Power III
d. Derived demand

3. _________ refers to a business or organization attempting to acquire goods or services to accomplish the goals of the enterprise. Though there are several organizations that attempt to set standards in the _________ process, processes can vary greatly between organizations. Typically the word '_________' is not used interchangeably with the word 'procurement', since procurement typically includes Expediting, Supplier Quality, and Traffic and Logistics (T'L) in addition to _________.

a. Supply network
b. Supply chain
c. Purchasing
d. Drop shipping

4. In economics, _________ is the desire to own something and the ability to pay for it. The term _________ signifies the ability or the willingness to buy a particular commodity at a given point of time .

a. Discretionary spending
b. Market system
c. Demand
d. Market dominance

5. _________ is a concept that denotes the precise probability of specific eventualities. Technically, the notion of _________ is independent from the notion of value and, as such, eventualities may have both beneficial and adverse consequences. However, in general usage the convention is to focus only on potential negative impact to some characteristic of value that may arise from a future event.

a. 6-3-5 Brainwriting
b. Power III
c. Risk
d. 180SearchAssistant

6. _________ is a term used in business to describe the process of capturing a customer's requirements. Specifically, the _________ is a market research technique that produces a detailed set of customer wants and needs, organized into a hierarchical structure, and then prioritized in terms of relative importance and satisfaction with current alternatives. _________ studies typically consist of both qualitative and quantitative research steps.

a. Digital strategy
b. Corporate transparency
c. Crisis management
d. Voice of the Customer

7. _________ is systematic determination of merit, worth, and significance of something or someone using criteria against a set of standards. _________ often is used to characterize and appraise subjects of interest in a wide range of human enterprises, including the arts, criminal justice, foundations and non-profit organizations, government, health care, and other human services.

Depending on the topic of interest, there are professional groups which look to the quality and rigor of the _________ process.

a. AMAX
b. ACNielsen
c. Evaluation
d. ADTECH

8. In economics, an externality or spillover of an economic transaction is an impact on a party that is not directly involved in the transaction. In such a case, prices do not reflect the full costs or benefits in production or consumption of a product or service. A positive impact is called an _________ benefit, while a negative impact is called an _________ cost.

a. ADTECH
b. AMAX
c. ACNielsen
d. External

9. _________ describes the situation when output from (or information about the result of) an event or phenomenon in the past will influence the same event/phenomenon in the present or future. When an event is part of a chain of cause-and-effect that forms a circuit or loop, then the event is said to 'feed back' into itself.

_________ is also a synonym for:

- _________ Signal; the information about the initial event that is the basis for subsequent modification of the event.
- _________ Loop; the causal path that leads from the initial generation of the _________ signal to the subsequent modification of the event.

_________ is a mechanism, process or signal that is looped back to control a system within itself. Such a loop is called a _________ loop.

a. 6-3-5 Brainwriting
b. Feedback
c. Power III
d. 180SearchAssistant

10. A _________ is an explicit set of requirements to be satisfied by a material, product, or service.

In engineering, manufacturing, and business, it is vital for suppliers, purchasers, and users of materials, products, or services to understand and agree upon all requirements. A _________ is a type of a standard which is often referenced by a contract or procurement document.

a. New product development
b. Product optimization
c. Product development
d. Specification

11. A supply chain is the system of organizations, people, technology, activities, information and resources involved in moving a product or service from _________ to customer. Supply chain activities transform natural resources, raw materials and components into a finished product that is delivered to the end customer. In sophisticated supply chain systems, used products may re-enter the supply chain at any point where residual value is recyclable.
a. Bringin' Home the Oil
b. Rebate
c. Supplier
d. Product line extension

12. Competitiveness is a comparative concept of the ability and performance of a firm, sub-sector or country to sell and supply goods and/or services in a given market. Although widely used in economics and business management, the usefulness of the concept, particularly in the context of national competitiveness, is vigorously disputed by economists, such as Paul Krugman .

The term may also be applied to markets, where it is used to refer to the extent to which the market structure may be regarded as perfectly _________.

a. Customs union
b. Competitive
c. Free trade zone
d. Geographical pricing

13. _________ is a form of assessment in which respondents are asked to select one or more choices from a list. The _________ format is most frequently used in educational testing, in market research, and in elections-- when a person chooses between multiple candidates, parties, or policies. _________ testing is particularly popular in the United States.

a. 180SearchAssistant
b. 6-3-5 Brainwriting
c. Power III
d. Multiple choice

14. _________ refers to the structured transmission of data between organizations by electronic means. It is used to transfer electronic documents from one computer system to another (ie) from one trading partner to another trading partner. It is more than mere E-mail; for instance, organizations might replace bills of lading and even checks with appropriate _________ messages.

a. Electronic data interchange
b. AMAX
c. ACNielsen
d. ADTECH

15. A _________, in marketing, procurement, and organizational studies, is a group of employees, family members, or members of any type of organization responsible for purchasing an item for the organization. In a business setting, major purchases typically require input from various parts of the organization, including finance, accounting, purchasing, information technology management, and senior management. Highly technical purchases, such as information systems or production equipment, also require the expertise of technical specialists.

a. Commercialization
b. Packshot
c. Buying center
d. Marketing myopia

16. _________ refer to a collection of facts usually collected as the result of experience, observation or experiment or a set of premises. This may consist of numbers, words particularly as measurements or observations of a set of variables. _________ are often viewed as a lowest level of abstraction from which information and knowledge are derived.

a. Pearson product-moment correlation coefficient
b. Data
c. Sample size
d. Mean

17. Electronic commerce, commonly known as _________ or eCommerce, consists of the buying and selling of products or services over electronic systems such as the Internet and other computer networks. The amount of trade conducted electronically has grown extraordinarily with wide-spread Internet usage. A wide variety of commerce is conducted in this way, spurring and drawing on innovations in electronic funds transfer, supply chain management, Internet marketing, online transaction processing, electronic data interchange (EDI), inventory management systems, and automated data collection systems.

a. ADTECH
b. AMAX
c. ACNielsen
d. E-commerce

18. _________ is defined by communication scholars in numerous ways, usually describing participants who are dependent upon one another and have a shared history. Communication channels, the conceptualization of mediums that carry messages from sender to receiver, take two distinct forms: direct and indirect.

Direct channels are obvious and easily recognized by the receiver.

a. AMAX
b. ACNielsen
c. ADTECH
d. Interpersonal communication

19. _________ is a recursive process where two or more people or organizations work together toward an intersection of common goals -- for example, an intellectual endeavor that is creative in nature--by sharing knowledge, learning and building consensus. _________ does not require leadership and can sometimes bring better results through decentralization and egalitarianism. In particular, teams that work collaboratively can obtain greater resources, recognition and reward when facing competition for finite resources._________ is also present in opposing goals exhibiting the notion of adversarial _________, though this notion is atypical of the annotation that people have given towards their understanding of _________.

a. 6-3-5 Brainwriting
b. 180SearchAssistant
c. Collaboration
d. Power III

20. _________ is subcontracting a process, such as product design or manufacturing, to a third-party company. The decision to outsource is often made in the interest of lowering cost or making better use of time and energy costs, redirecting or conserving energy directed at the competencies of a particular business, or to make more efficient use of land, labor, capital, (information) technology and resources. _________ became part of the business lexicon during the 1980s.

a. ACNielsen
b. In-house
c. Intangible assets
d. Outsourcing

21. A _________ or logistics network is the system of organizations, people, technology, activities, information and resources involved in moving a product or service from supplier to customer. _________ activities transform natural resources, raw materials and components into a finished product that is delivered to the end customer. In sophisticated _________ systems, used products may re-enter the _________ at any point where residual value is recyclable.

a. Purchasing
b. Supply chain network
c. Demand chain management
d. Supply chain

22. _________ is one of the four Ps of the marketing mix. The other three aspects are product, promotion, and place. It is also a key variable in microeconomic price allocation theory.

a. Price
b. Relationship based pricing
c. Pricing
d. Competitor indexing

1. _________ is the physical search for minerals, fossils, precious metals or mineral specimens, and is also known as fossicking.

_________ is synonymous in some ways with mineral exploration which is an organised, large scale and at least semi-scientific effort undertaken by mineral resource companies to find commercially viable ore deposits. To actually be considered a prospector you must become registered as a professional prospector.

a. Prospecting
b. Power III
c. 180SearchAssistant
d. 6-3-5 Brainwriting

2. _________ is a recursive process where two or more people or organizations work together toward an intersection of common goals -- for example, an intellectual endeavor that is creative in nature--by sharing knowledge, learning and building consensus. _________ does not require leadership and can sometimes bring better results through decentralization and egalitarianism. In particular, teams that work collaboratively can obtain greater resources, recognition and reward when facing competition for finite resources._________ is also present in opposing goals exhibiting the notion of adversarial _________, though this notion is atypical of the annotation that people have given towards their understanding of _________.

a. 6-3-5 Brainwriting
b. Collaboration
c. Power III
d. 180SearchAssistant

3. _________ is a branch of philosophy which seeks to address questions about morality, such as how a moral outcome can be achieved in a specific situation (applied _________), how moral values should be determined (normative _________), what moral values people actually abide by (descriptive _________), what the fundamental semantic, ontological, and epistemic nature of _________ or morality is (meta-_________), and how moral capacity or moral agency develops and what its nature is (moral psychology.)

Socrates was one of the first Greek philosophers to encourage both scholars and the common citizen to turn their attention from the outside world to the condition of man. In this view, Knowledge having a bearing on human life was placed highest, all other knowledge being secondary.

a. ACNielsen
b. Ethics
c. AMAX
d. ADTECH

4. _________ is difficult to define. For example, in 1952, Alfred Kroeber and Clyde Kluckhohn compiled a list of 164 definitions of '_________' in _________: A Critical Review of Concepts and Definitions. However, the word '_________' is most commonly used in three basic senses:

- excellence of taste in the fine arts and humanities
- an integrated pattern of human knowledge, belief, and behavior that depends upon the capacity for symbolic thought and social learning
- the set of shared attitudes, values, goals, and practices that characterizes an institution, organization or group.

When the concept first emerged in eighteenth- and nineteenth-century Europe, it connoted a process of cultivation or improvement, as in agriculture or horticulture. In the nineteenth century, it came to refer first to the betterment or refinement of the individual, especially through education, and then to the fulfillment of national aspirations or ideals.

a. African Americans
b. AStore
c. Albert Einstein
d. Culture

5. _________ is defined by communication scholars in numerous ways, usually describing participants who are dependent upon one another and have a shared history. Communication channels, the conceptualization of mediums that carry messages from sender to receiver, take two distinct forms: direct and indirect.

Direct channels are obvious and easily recognized by the receiver.

a. ADTECH
b. Interpersonal communication
c. ACNielsen
d. AMAX

6. _________ is the identity of a group or culture, or of an individual as far as one is influenced by one's belonging to a group or culture. _________ is similar to and has overlaps with, but is not synonymous with, identity politics.

There are modern questions of culture that are transferred into questions of identity.

a. 6-3-5 Brainwriting
b. Power III
c. Cultural identity
d. 180SearchAssistant

7. Electronic commerce, commonly known as _________ or eCommerce, consists of the buying and selling of products or services over electronic systems such as the Internet and other computer networks. The amount of trade conducted electronically has grown extraordinarily with wide-spread Internet usage. A wide variety of commerce is conducted in this way, spurring and drawing on innovations in electronic funds transfer, supply chain management, Internet marketing, online transaction processing, electronic data interchange (EDI), inventory management systems, and automated data collection systems.

a. ACNielsen
b. AMAX
c. ADTECH
d. E-Commerce

8. _________ is systematic determination of merit, worth, and significance of something or someone using criteria against a set of standards. _________ often is used to characterize and appraise subjects of interest in a wide range of human enterprises, including the arts, criminal justice, foundations and non-profit organizations, government, health care, and other human services.

Depending on the topic of interest, there are professional groups which look to the quality and rigor of the _________ process.

a. ACNielsen
b. AMAX
c. Evaluation
d. ADTECH

1. _________ is the physical search for minerals, fossils, precious metals or mineral specimens, and is also known as fossicking.

_________ is synonymous in some ways with mineral exploration which is an organised, large scale and at least semi-scientific effort undertaken by mineral resource companies to find commercially viable ore deposits. To actually be considered a prospector you must become registered as a professional prospector.

a. 180SearchAssistant
b. Power III
c. Prospecting
d. 6-3-5 Brainwriting

2. An _________ is a special-purpose computer system designed to perform one or a few dedicated functions, often with real-time computing constraints. It is usually embedded as part of a complete device including hardware and mechanical parts. In contrast, a general-purpose computer, such as a personal computer, can do many different tasks depending on programming.
a. AMAX
b. ADTECH
c. ACNielsen
d. Embedded system

3. In economics, an externality or spillover of an economic transaction is an impact on a party that is not directly involved in the transaction. In such a case, prices do not reflect the full costs or benefits in production or consumption of a product or service. A positive impact is called an _________ benefit, while a negative impact is called an _________ cost.
a. ADTECH
b. ACNielsen
c. AMAX
d. External

4. _________ is the practice of individuals including commercial businesses, governments and institutions, facilitating the sale of their products or services to other companies or organizations that in turn resell them, use them as components in products or services they offer _________ is also called business-to-_________ for short. (Note that while marketing to government entities shares some of the same dynamics of organizational marketing, B2G Marketing is meaningfully different.)
a. Disruptive technology
b. Mass marketing
c. Business marketing
d. Law of disruption

5. _________ is a form of communication that typically attempts to persuade potential customers to purchase or to consume more of a particular brand of product or service. 'While now central to the contemporary global economy and the reproduction of global production networks, it is only quite recently that _________ has been more than a marginal influence on patterns of sales and production. The formation of modern _________ was intimately bound up with the emergence of new forms of monopoly capitalism around the end of the 19th and beginning of the 20th century as one element in corporate strategies to create, organize and where possible control markets, especially for mass produced consumer goods.

a. Advertising
b. ADTECH
c. AMAX
d. ACNielsen

6. _________ is the provision of service to customers before, during and after a purchase.

According to Turban et al., '_________ is a series of activities designed to enhance the level of customer satisfaction - that is, the feeling that a product or service has met the customer expectation.'

Its importance varies by product, industry and customer.

a. Facing
b. Customer experience
c. COPC Inc.
d. Customer service

7. _________ is an advertisement in which a particular product specifically mentions a competitor by name for the express purpose of showing why the competitor is inferior to the product naming it.

This should not be confused with parody advertisements, where a fictional product is being advertised for the purpose of poking fun at the particular advertisement, nor should it be confused with the use of a coined brand name for the purpose of comparing the product without actually naming an actual competitor. ('Wikipedia tastes better and is less filling than the Encyclopedia Galactica.')

In the 1980s, during what has been referred to as the cola wars, soft-drink manufacturer Pepsi ran a series of advertisements where people, caught on hidden camera, in a blind taste test, chose Pepsi over rival Coca-Cola.

a. Cost per conversion
b. Comparative advertising
c. Heavy-up
d. GL-70

8. A _________ is a structured collection of records or data that is stored in a computer system. The structure is achieved by organizing the data according to a _________ model. The model in most common use today is the relational model.

a. Database
b. 6-3-5 Brainwriting
c. Power III
d. 180SearchAssistant

9. _________ is defined by the American _________ Association as the activity, set of institutions, and processes for creating, communicating, delivering, and exchanging offerings that have value for customers, clients, partners, and society at large. The term developed from the original meaning which referred literally to going to market, as in shopping, or going to a market to sell goods or services.

_________ practice tends to be seen as a creative industry, which includes advertising, distribution and selling.

a. Product naming
b. Marketing
c. Customer acquisition management
d. Marketing myopia

10. _________ is a business discipline which is focused on the practical application of marketing techniques and the management of a firm's marketing resources and activities. Marketing managers are often responsible for influencing the level, timing, and composition of customer demand accepted definition of the term. In part, this is because the role of a marketing manager can vary significantly based on a business' size, corporate culture, and industry context.

a. Door-to-door
b. Performance-based advertising
c. Business structure
d. Marketing Management

11. A trade fair (trade show or expo) is an exhibition organized so that companies in a specific industry can showcase and demonstrate their latest products, service, study activities of rivals and examine recent trends and opportunities. Some trade fairs are open to the public, while others can only be attended by company representatives (members of the trade) and members of the press, therefore _________ are classified as either 'Public' or 'Trade Only'. They are held on a continuing basis in virtually all markets and normally attract companies from around the globe.

a. 180SearchAssistant
b. Power III
c. 6-3-5 Brainwriting
d. Trade Shows

12. A _________ is a relatively new executive level position at a corporation, company, organization typically reporting directly to the CEO or board of directors. The _________ is responsible for a brand's image, experience, and promise, and propagating it throughout all aspects of the company. The brand officer oversees marketing, advertising, design, public relations and customer service departments.

a. Financial analyst
b. Chief executive officer
c. Power III
d. Chief brand officer

13. _________ is a method of direct marketing in which a salesperson solicits to prospective customers to buy products or services, either over the phone or through a subsequent face to face or Web conferencing appointment scheduled during the call.

_________ can also include recorded sales pitches programmed to be played over the phone via automatic dialing. _________ has come under fire in recent years, being viewed as an annoyance by many.

a. Telemarketing
b. Joe job
c. Directory Harvest Attack
d. Phishing

14. The _________ is a very large set of interlinked hypertext documents accessed via the Internet. With a Web browser, one can view Web pages that may contain text, images, videos, and other multimedia and navigate between them using hyperlinks. Using concepts from earlier hypertext systems, the _________ was begun in 1992 by the English physicist Sir Tim Berners-Lee, now the Director of the _________ Consortium, and Robert Cailliau, a Belgian computer scientist, while both were working at CERN in Geneva, Switzerland.

a. World Wide Web
b. 180SearchAssistant
c. 6-3-5 Brainwriting
d. Power III

15. _________ is either an activity of a living being (such as a human), consisting of receiving knowledge of the outside world through the senses, or the recording of data using scientific instruments. The term may also refer to any datum collected during this activity.

The scientific method requires _________s of nature to formulate and test hypotheses.

a. ADTECH
b. AMAX
c. Observation
d. ACNielsen

16. _________ is a term used in business to describe the process of capturing a customer's requirements. Specifically, the _________ is a market research technique that produces a detailed set of customer wants and needs, organized into a hierarchical structure, and then prioritized in terms of relative importance and satisfaction with current alternatives. _________ studies typically consist of both qualitative and quantitative research steps.

a. Crisis management
b. Voice of the Customer
c. Digital strategy
d. Corporate transparency

1. _________ in organizations and public policy is both the organizational process of creating and maintaining a plan; and the psychological process of thinking about the activities required to create a desired goal on some scale. As such, it is a fundamental property of intelligent behavior. This thought process is essential to the creation and refinement of a plan, or integration of it with other plans, that is, it combines forecasting of developments with the preparation of scenarios of how to react to them.

a. Power III
b. 6-3-5 Brainwriting
c. 180SearchAssistant
d. Planning

2. _________ is an advertisement in which a particular product specifically mentions a competitor by name for the express purpose of showing why the competitor is inferior to the product naming it.

This should not be confused with parody advertisements, where a fictional product is being advertised for the purpose of poking fun at the particular advertisement, nor should it be confused with the use of a coined brand name for the purpose of comparing the product without actually naming an actual competitor. ('Wikipedia tastes better and is less filling than the Encyclopedia Galactica.')

In the 1980s, during what has been referred to as the cola wars, soft-drink manufacturer Pepsi ran a series of advertisements where people, caught on hidden camera, in a blind taste test, chose Pepsi over rival Coca-Cola.

a. Cost per conversion
b. GL-70
c. Comparative advertising
d. Heavy-up

3. A _________ is an invitation for suppliers, often through a bidding process, to submit a proposal on a specific commodity or service. A bidding process is one of the best methods for leveraging a company's negotiating ability and purchasing power with suppliers. The _________ process brings structure to the procurement decision and allows the risks and benefits to be identified clearly upfront.

a. Hit rate
b. Lead generation
c. Sales management
d. Request for proposal

4. _________ in economics and business is the result of an exchange and from that trade we assign a numerical monetary value to a good, service or asset. If I trade 4 apples for an orange, the _________ of an orange is 4 - apples. Inversely, the _________ of an apple is 1/4 oranges.

a. Contribution margin-based pricing
b. Price
c. Pricing
d. Discounts and allowances

5. _________ is one of the four Ps of the marketing mix. The other three aspects are product, promotion, and place. It is also a key variable in microeconomic price allocation theory.
a. Competitor indexing
b. Price
c. Relationship based pricing
d. Pricing

6. _________ is a rivalry between individuals, groups, nations for territory, a niche, or allocation of resources. It arises whenever two or more parties strive for a goal which cannot be shared. _________ occurs naturally between living organisms which co-exist in the same environment.
a. Price competition
b. Non-price competition
c. Price fixing
d. Competition

7. In the United States , a _________ is the name commonly given to a private group, regardless of size, organized to elect political candidates. Legally, what constitutes a '_________' for purposes of regulation is a matter of state and federal law. Under the Federal Election Campaign Act, an organization becomes a 'political committee' by receiving contributions or making expenditures in excess of $1,000 for the purpose of influencing a federal election.
a. Political Action Committee
b. 180SearchAssistant
c. Power III
d. 6-3-5 Brainwriting

1. _________ is defined by the American _________ Association as the activity, set of institutions, and processes for creating, communicating, delivering, and exchanging offerings that have value for customers, clients, partners, and society at large. The term developed from the original meaning which referred literally to going to market, as in shopping, or going to a market to sell goods or services.

_________ practice tends to be seen as a creative industry, which includes advertising, distribution and selling.

a. Marketing
b. Product naming
c. Marketing myopia
d. Customer acquisition management

2. _________ is a business discipline which is focused on the practical application of marketing techniques and the management of a firm's marketing resources and activities. Marketing managers are often responsible for influencing the level, timing, and composition of customer demand accepted definition of the term. In part, this is because the role of a marketing manager can vary significantly based on a business' size, corporate culture, and industry context.
a. Performance-based advertising
b. Business structure
c. Door-to-door
d. Marketing Management

3. _________ involves disseminating information about a product, product line, brand, or company. It is one of the four key aspects of the marketing mix. (The other three elements are product marketing, pricing, and distribution). P>_________ is generally sub-divided into two parts:

- Above the line _________: Promotion in the media (e.g. TV, radio, newspapers, Internet and Mobile Phones) in which the advertiser pays an advertising agency to place the ad
- Below the line _________: All other _________. Much of this is intended to be subtle enough for the consumer to be unaware that _________ is taking place. E.g. sponsorship, product placement, endorsements, sales _________, merchandising, direct mail, personal selling, public relations, trade shows

a. Promotion
b. Cashmere Agency
c. Davie Brown Index
d. Bottling lines

4. A personal and cultural _________ is a relative ethic _________, an assumption upon which implementation can be extrapolated. A _________ system is a set of consistent _________s and measures that is soo not true. A principle _________ is a foundation upon which other _________s and measures of integrity are based.

a. Supreme Court of the United States
b. Value
c. Perceptual maps
d. Package-on-Package

5. In the field of marketing, a customer _________ consists of the sum total of benefits which a vendor promises that a customer will receive in return for the customer's associated payment (or other value-transfer.)

Put simply, the _________ is what the customer gets for his money.

Accordingly, a customer can evaluate a company's value-proposition on two broad dimensions with multiple subsets:

1. relative performance: what the customer gets from the vendor relative to a competitor's offering;
2. price: which consists of the payment the customer makes to acquire the product or service; plus the access cost

The vendor-company's marketing and sales efforts offer a customer _________; the vendor-company's delivery and customer-service processes then fulfill that value-proposition.

A value-proposition can assist in a firm's marketing strategy, and may guide a business to target a particular market segment.

a. Marketing performance measurement and management
b. Relationship management
c. DefCom Australia
d. Value proposition

6. In marketing, _________ has come to mean the process by which marketers try to create an image or identity in the minds of their target market for its product, brand, or organization. It is the 'relative competitive comparison' their product occupies in a given market as perceived by the target market.

Re-_________ involves changing the identity of a product, relative to the identity of competing products, in the collective minds of the target market.

a. Containerization
b. GE matrix
c. Moratorium
d. Positioning

7. _________ is a mathematical science pertaining to the collection, analysis, interpretation or explanation, and presentation of data. It also provides tools for prediction and forecasting based on data. It is applicable to a wide variety of academic disciplines, from the natural and social sciences to the humanities, government and business.

a. Type I error
b. Median
c. Null hypothesis
d. Statistics

8. In promotion and of advertising, a _________ or endorsement consists of a written or spoken statement, sometimes from a person figure, sometimes from a private citizen, extolling the virtue of some product. The term '_________' most commonly applies to the sales-pitches attributed to ordinary citizens, whereas 'endorsement' usually applies to pitches by celebrities. See also Testify, Testimony, for historical context and etymology.

a. Roll-in
b. Promotional products
c. Transpromotional
d. Testimonial

9. _________ is a recursive process where two or more people or organizations work together toward an intersection of common goals -- for example, an intellectual endeavor that is creative in nature--by sharing knowledge, learning and building consensus. _________ does not require leadership and can sometimes bring better results through decentralization and egalitarianism. In particular, teams that work collaboratively can obtain greater resources, recognition and reward when facing competition for finite resources._________ is also present in opposing goals exhibiting the notion of adversarial _________, though this notion is atypical of the annotation that people have given towards their understanding of _________.

a. Power III
b. 180SearchAssistant
c. 6-3-5 Brainwriting
d. Collaboration

1. _________ is the physical search for minerals, fossils, precious metals or mineral specimens, and is also known as fossicking.

_________ is synonymous in some ways with mineral exploration which is an organised, large scale and at least semi-scientific effort undertaken by mineral resource companies to find commercially viable ore deposits. To actually be considered a prospector you must become registered as a professional prospector.

a. Power III
b. 180SearchAssistant
c. Prospecting
d. 6-3-5 Brainwriting

2. _________ in economics and business is the result of an exchange and from that trade we assign a numerical monetary value to a good, service or asset. If I trade 4 apples for an orange, the _________ of an orange is 4 - apples. Inversely, the _________ of an apple is 1/4 oranges.

a. Pricing
b. Discounts and allowances
c. Contribution margin-based pricing
d. Price

3. _________ is an advertisement in which a particular product specifically mentions a competitor by name for the express purpose of showing why the competitor is inferior to the product naming it.

This should not be confused with parody advertisements, where a fictional product is being advertised for the purpose of poking fun at the particular advertisement, nor should it be confused with the use of a coined brand name for the purpose of comparing the product without actually naming an actual competitor. ('Wikipedia tastes better and is less filling than the Encyclopedia Galactica.')

In the 1980s, during what has been referred to as the cola wars, soft-drink manufacturer Pepsi ran a series of advertisements where people, caught on hidden camera, in a blind taste test, chose Pepsi over rival Coca-Cola.

a. GL-70
b. Cost per conversion
c. Comparative advertising
d. Heavy-up

4. In operant conditioning, _________ occurs when an event following a response causes an increase in the probability of that response occurring in the future. Response strength can be assessed by measures such as the frequency with which the response is made (for example, a pigeon may peck a key more times in the session), or the speed with which it is made (for example, a rat may run a maze faster.) The environment change contingent upon the response is called a reinforcer.

a. Completely randomized designs
b. Generic brands
c. Reinforcement
d. Relationship Management Application

5. In marketing language, a _________ is a unique or quirky special feature that makes something 'stand out' from its contemporaries. However, the special feature is typically thought to be of little relevance or use. Thus, a _________ is a special feature for the sake of having a special feature.
a. Customer Interaction Tracker
b. Marketing plan
c. Prosumer
d. Gimmick

6. A _________ is a type of business entity in which partners (owners) share with each other the profits or losses of the business undertaking in which all have invested. _________s are often favored over corporations for taxation purposes, as the _________ structure does not generally incur a tax on profits before it is distributed to the partners (i.e. there is no dividend tax levied.) However, depending on the _________ structure and the jurisdiction in which it operates, owners of a _________ may be exposed to greater personal liability than they would as shareholders of a corporation.
a. Fair Debt Collection Practices Act
b. Brand piracy
c. Partnership
d. Competition law

1. _________ is the set of reasons that determines one to engage in a particular behavior. The term is generally used for human _________ but, theoretically, it can be used to describe the causes for animal behavior as well

a. Role playing
b. Power III
c. 180SearchAssistant
d. Motivation

2. A _________ is a systematic approach to selling a product or service. A growing body of published literature approaches the _________ from the point of view of an engineering discipline

Reasons for having a well thought-out _________ include seller and buyer risk management, standardized customer interaction in sales, and scalable revenue generation.

a. Request for proposal
b. Lead generation
c. Sales management
d. Sales process

3. _________, a business term, is a measure of how products and services supplied by a company meet or surpass customer expectation. It is seen as a key performance indicator within business and is part of the four perspectives of a Balanced Scorecard.

In a competitive marketplace where businesses compete for customers, _________ is seen as a key differentiator and increasingly has become a key element of business strategy.

a. Supplier diversity
b. Customer satisfaction
c. Customer base
d. Psychological pricing

4. _________ is the provision of service to customers before, during and after a purchase.

According to Turban et al., '_________ is a series of activities designed to enhance the level of customer satisfaction - that is, the feeling that a product or service has met the customer expectation.'

Its importance varies by product, industry and customer.

a. Customer experience
b. COPC Inc.
c. Facing
d. Customer service

5. _________ is an advertisement in which a particular product specifically mentions a competitor by name for the express purpose of showing why the competitor is inferior to the product naming it.

This should not be confused with parody advertisements, where a fictional product is being advertised for the purpose of poking fun at the particular advertisement, nor should it be confused with the use of a coined brand name for the purpose of comparing the product without actually naming an actual competitor. ('Wikipedia tastes better and is less filling than the Encyclopedia Galactica.')

In the 1980s, during what has been referred to as the cola wars, soft-drink manufacturer Pepsi ran a series of advertisements where people, caught on hidden camera, in a blind taste test, chose Pepsi over rival Coca-Cola.

a. Comparative advertising
b. Cost per conversion
c. Heavy-up
d. GL-70

6. A personal and cultural _________ is a relative ethic _________, an assumption upon which implementation can be extrapolated. A _________ system is a set of consistent _________s and measures that is soo not true. A principle _________ is a foundation upon which other _________s and measures of integrity are based.
a. Perceptual maps
b. Package-on-Package
c. Supreme Court of the United States
d. Value

7. _________ is the activity that the selling organization undertakes to reduce customer account defections. The success of this activity is when the customer account places an additional order before a 12-month period has expired. Note that ideally these orders will need to contribute similar financial amounts to the previous 12 months.
a. Customer centricity
b. Customer retention
c. First-mover advantage
d. Customer base

8. A _________ is a structured collection of records or data that is stored in a computer system. The structure is achieved by organizing the data according to a _________ model. The model in most common use today is the relational model.

a. Database
b. 6-3-5 Brainwriting
c. Power III
d. 180SearchAssistant

9. An _________ is a private network that uses Internet protocols, network connectivity, and possibly the public telecommunication system to securely share part of an organization's information or operations with suppliers, vendors, partners, customers or other businesses. An _________ can be viewed as part of a company's intranet that is extended to users outside the company (e.g.: normally over the Internet.) It has also been described as a 'state of mind' in which the Internet is perceived as a way to do business with a preapproved set of other companies business-to-business (B2B), in isolation from all other Internet users.

a. ACNielsen
b. AMAX
c. ADTECH
d. Extranet

10. _________ operations or facilities are commonly called 'distribution centers'. '_________' is the term generally used to describe the process or the work flow associated with the picking, packing and delivery of the packed item(s) to a shipping carrier.

a. ADTECH
b. ACNielsen
c. Order processing
d. AMAX

11. _________ is a recursive process where two or more people or organizations work together toward an intersection of common goals -- for example, an intellectual endeavor that is creative in nature--by sharing knowledge, learning and building consensus. _________ does not require leadership and can sometimes bring better results through decentralization and egalitarianism. In particular, teams that work collaboratively can obtain greater resources, recognition and reward when facing competition for finite resources._________ is also present in opposing goals exhibiting the notion of adversarial _________, though this notion is atypical of the annotation that people have given towards their understanding of _________.

a. Power III
b. 180SearchAssistant
c. 6-3-5 Brainwriting
d. Collaboration

12. _________ is anything that is intended to save time, energy or frustration. A _________ store at a petrol station, for example, sells items that have nothing to do with gasoline/petrol, but it saves the consumer from having to go to a grocery store. '_________' is a very relative term and its meaning tends to change over time.

a. Marketing buzz
b. MaxDiff
c. Demographic profile
d. Convenience

13. _________ describes the situation when output from (or information about the result of) an event or phenomenon in the past will influence the same event/phenomenon in the present or future. When an event is part of a chain of cause-and-effect that forms a circuit or loop, then the event is said to 'feed back' into itself.

_________ is also a synonym for:

- _________ Signal; the information about the initial event that is the basis for subsequent modification of the event.
- _________ Loop; the causal path that leads from the initial generation of the _________ signal to the subsequent modification of the event.

_________ is a mechanism, process or signal that is looped back to control a system within itself. Such a loop is called a _________ loop.

a. 6-3-5 Brainwriting
b. Feedback
c. Power III
d. 180SearchAssistant

14. A _________ is a plan of action designed to achieve a particular goal.

_________ is different from tactics. In military terms, tactics is concerned with the conduct of an engagement while _________ is concerned with how different engagements are linked.

a. Power III
b. 180SearchAssistant
c. 6-3-5 Brainwriting
d. Strategy

1. _________ is the activity that the selling organization undertakes to reduce customer account defections. The success of this activity is when the customer account places an additional order before a 12-month period has expired. Note that ideally these orders will need to contribute similar financial amounts to the previous 12 months.

a. Customer base
b. Customer retention
c. First-mover advantage
d. Customer centricity

2. _________ is the provision of service to customers before, during and after a purchase.

According to Turban et al., '_________ is a series of activities designed to enhance the level of customer satisfaction - that is, the feeling that a product or service has met the customer expectation.'

Its importance varies by product, industry and customer.

a. COPC Inc.
b. Facing
c. Customer experience
d. Customer service

3. _________, in strategic management and marketing, is the percentage or proportion of the total available market or market segment that is being serviced by a company. It can be expressed as a company's sales revenue (from that market) divided by the total sales revenue available in that market. It can also be expressed as a company's unit sales volume (in a market) divided by the total volume of units sold in that market.

a. Cyberdoc
b. Customer relationship management
c. Demand generation
d. Market share

4. In accounting, _________ has a very specific meaning. It is an outflow of cash or other valuable assets from a person or company to another person or company. This outflow of cash is generally one side of a trade for products or services that have equal or better current or future value to the buyer than to the seller.

a. AMAX
b. ADTECH
c. Expense
d. ACNielsen

5. _________ describes the situation when output from (or information about the result of) an event or phenomenon in the past will influence the same event/phenomenon in the present or future. When an event is part of a chain of cause-and-effect that forms a circuit or loop, then the event is said to 'feed back' into itself.

_________ is also a synonym for:

- _________ Signal; the information about the initial event that is the basis for subsequent modification of the event.
- _________ Loop; the causal path that leads from the initial generation of the _________ signal to the subsequent modification of the event.

_________ is a mechanism, process or signal that is looped back to control a system within itself. Such a loop is called a _________ loop.

a. 180SearchAssistant
b. Power III
c. 6-3-5 Brainwriting
d. Feedback

6. _________ is an advertisement in which a particular product specifically mentions a competitor by name for the express purpose of showing why the competitor is inferior to the product naming it.

This should not be confused with parody advertisements, where a fictional product is being advertised for the purpose of poking fun at the particular advertisement, nor should it be confused with the use of a coined brand name for the purpose of comparing the product without actually naming an actual competitor. ('Wikipedia tastes better and is less filling than the Encyclopedia Galactica.')

In the 1980s, during what has been referred to as the cola wars, soft-drink manufacturer Pepsi ran a series of advertisements where people, caught on hidden camera, in a blind taste test, chose Pepsi over rival Coca-Cola.

a. Comparative advertising
b. GL-70
c. Heavy-up
d. Cost per conversion

7. _________ in organizations and public policy is both the organizational process of creating and maintaining a plan; and the psychological process of thinking about the activities required to create a desired goal on some scale. As such, it is a fundamental property of intelligent behavior. This thought process is essential to the creation and refinement of a plan, or integration of it with other plans, that is, it combines forecasting of developments with the preparation of scenarios of how to react to them.

a. 6-3-5 Brainwriting
b. Power III
c. 180SearchAssistant
d. Planning

8. A _________ is a plan of action designed to achieve a particular goal.

_________ is different from tactics. In military terms, tactics is concerned with the conduct of an engagement while _________ is concerned with how different engagements are linked.

a. Power III
b. Strategy
c. 6-3-5 Brainwriting
d. 180SearchAssistant

9. A _________ is a structured collection of records or data that is stored in a computer system. The structure is achieved by organizing the data according to a _________ model. The model in most common use today is the relational model.
a. Power III
b. 180SearchAssistant
c. 6-3-5 Brainwriting
d. Database

10. An _________ is a private network that uses Internet protocols, network connectivity, and possibly the public telecommunication system to securely share part of an organization's information or operations with suppliers, vendors, partners, customers or other businesses. An _________ can be viewed as part of a company's intranet that is extended to users outside the company (e.g.: normally over the Internet.) It has also been described as a 'state of mind' in which the Internet is perceived as a way to do business with a preapproved set of other companies business-to-business (B2B), in isolation from all other Internet users.
a. AMAX
b. ADTECH
c. ACNielsen
d. Extranet

11. _________ is defined by the American _________ Association as the activity, set of institutions, and processes for creating, communicating, delivering, and exchanging offerings that have value for customers, clients, partners, and society at large. The term developed from the original meaning which referred literally to going to market, as in shopping, or going to a market to sell goods or services.

_________ practice tends to be seen as a creative industry, which includes advertising, distribution and selling.

a. Marketing
b. Marketing myopia
c. Product naming
d. Customer acquisition management

12. The _________ is a very large set of interlinked hypertext documents accessed via the Internet. With a Web browser, one can view Web pages that may contain text, images, videos, and other multimedia and navigate between them using hyperlinks. Using concepts from earlier hypertext systems, the _________ was begun in 1992 by the English physicist Sir Tim Berners-Lee, now the Director of the _________ Consortium, and Robert Cailliau, a Belgian computer scientist, while both were working at CERN in Geneva, Switzerland.

a. 180SearchAssistant
b. 6-3-5 Brainwriting
c. Power III
d. World Wide Web

13. A _________ is a type of business entity in which partners (owners) share with each other the profits or losses of the business undertaking in which all have invested. _________s are often favored over corporations for taxation purposes, as the _________ structure does not generally incur a tax on profits before it is distributed to the partners (i.e. there is no dividend tax levied.) However, depending on the _________ structure and the jurisdiction in which it operates, owners of a _________ may be exposed to greater personal liability than they would as shareholders of a corporation.

a. Brand piracy
b. Competition law
c. Partnership
d. Fair Debt Collection Practices Act

14. In economics, an externality or spillover of an economic transaction is an impact on a party that is not directly involved in the transaction. In such a case, prices do not reflect the full costs or benefits in production or consumption of a product or service. A positive impact is called an _________ benefit, while a negative impact is called an _________ cost.

a. AMAX
b. External
c. ACNielsen
d. ADTECH

15. Competitiveness is a comparative concept of the ability and performance of a firm, sub-sector or country to sell and supply goods and/or services in a given market. Although widely used in economics and business management, the usefulness of the concept, particularly in the context of national competitiveness, is vigorously disputed by economists, such as Paul Krugman .

The term may also be applied to markets, where it is used to refer to the extent to which the market structure may be regarded as perfectly _________.

a. Geographical pricing
b. Customs union
c. Competitive
d. Free trade zone

Chapter 1

1. b	2. d	3. d	4. c	5. b	6. c	7. a	8. d	9. a	10. a
11. d	12. d	13. d	14. d	15. d	16. d	17. d	18. c	19. d	20. a
21. d									

Chapter 2

1. b	2. c	3. d	4. b	5. c	6. d	7. b	8. a	9. b	10. a
11. c	12. a	13. d	14. d	15. d	16. d	17. d			

Chapter 3

1. d	2. d	3. c	4. c	5. c	6. d	7. c	8. d	9. b	10. d
11. c	12. b	13. d	14. a	15. c	16. b	17. d	18. d	19. c	20. d
21. d	22. c								

Chapter 4

1. a	2. b	3. b	4. d	5. b	6. c	7. d	8. c

Chapter 5

1. c	2. d	3. d	4. c	5. a	6. d	7. b	8. a	9. b	10. d
11. d	12. d	13. a	14. a	15. c	16. b				

Chapter 6

1. d	2. c	3. d	4. b	5. d	6. d	7. a

Chapter 7

1. a	2. d	3. a	4. b	5. d	6. d	7. d	8. d	9. d

Chapter 8

1. c	2. d	3. c	4. c	5. d	6. c

Chapter 9

1. d	2. d	3. b	4. d	5. a	6. d	7. b	8. a	9. d	10. c
11. d	12. d	13. b	14. d						

Chapter 10

1. b	2. d	3. d	4. c	5. d	6. a	7. d	8. b	9. d	10. d
11. a	12. d	13. c	14. b	15. c					

www.ingramcontent.com/pod-product-compliance
Lightning Source LLC
Chambersburg PA
CBHW080744250426
43671CB00038B/2868
* 9 7 8 1 4 2 8 8 7 3 2 5 4 *